BUILDING COMMUNITIES

BUILDING
COMMUNITIES
A Vision For A New Century

A Report of the Commission on the Future of Community Colleges

American Association of Community and Junior Colleges
National Center for Higher Education
Suite 410, One Dupont Circle, NW
Washington, D.C. 20036
(202) 293-7050

Copyright © 1988
Printed in the United States of America

ISBN #0-87117-182-1

CONTENTS

FOREWORD

The United States is in the midst of a nationwide movement focusing on excellence in every aspect of our educational system. In addition, we are intertwined in a rapidly shifting environment reflected in the changing population, the nature of work, and the link between education and the economy. The plethora of studies purported to report on excellence in education has made virtually no mention of the significant role and contribution of community, technical, and junior colleges—the largest branch of American higher education.

It has been 40 years since the Truman Commission on Higher Education developed groundbreaking recommendations on community colleges. In 1947, as its work was completed, there were 640 junior colleges in the United States enrolling 497,065 college credit students. Today there are 1,224 regionally accredited community, technical, and junior colleges enrolling over five million college credit students, while another four million students are enrolled in non-credit adult and continuing education programs.

In 1986, after four decades of tremendous growth in the community college movement set against an accelerating number of economic, cultural, and demographic shifts in our society, the Board of Directors of the American Association of Community and Junior Colleges determined that it was appropriate for the current generation of college leaders to take stock of the community college movement and develop recommendations to help these colleges move into the twenty-first century with wisdom and vitality. There is a tremendous diversity among community colleges throughout the country, but the AACJC Board believed that a national study aimed at the future would be instructive as each institution plans its course at the state and local levels.

Nineteen distinguished Americans were appointed to the AACJC Commission on the Future of the Community Colleges with the charge to study the history, assess the current status, and develop recommendations for the future of community, technical, and junior colleges. After 18 months of intensive study, public hearings, campus visits, and much debate, this Commission is reporting its findings.

AACJC is deeply indebted to Commission members for their wisdom, dedicated service, and commitment to the task. United States Senator Nancy Kassebaum of Kansas deserves special thanks for serving as honorary Chair of the Commission. Many thanks must be extended to Dr. Ernest Boyer, President of The Carnegie Foundation for the Advancement of Teaching, for his efforts as working Chair of the

Commission. Appreciation must go also to the Dallas County Community College Board of Trustees and former Chancellor R. Jan LeCroy for their support and for making it possible for Nancy Armes to serve as the Executive Director of the Commission. Dr. Armes has, from the very first, coordinated the work of the Commission and the responses of individual members, and has been strategically important in the completion of the project.

The Commission's research and administrative staff provided crucial information and resources, as did colleagues at AACJC. The project would not have been completed without assistance from several members of the Carnegie Foundation staff. Marla Ucelli deserves special mention for endless hours devoted to critiquing drafts, coordinating comments from Commissioners, and preparing the document for publication.

In addition, AACJC is indebted to many individuals and organizations for their contributions to this report. During the past year and a half, the Commission heard testimony from over 100 persons, including legislators, higher education professors, community college presidents, trustees, faculty, and students.

AACJC also owes a debt of gratitude to the following organizations whose generous support helped make the work of the Commission possible: Colgate Palmolive Company; Corn Products Corporation International, Inc.; Ford Motor Company Fund; General Foods Corporation; General Motors Corporation; IBM; Shell Oil Companies Foundation; and The New York Times Company Foundation, Inc.

With the assistance of these many individuals and groups, the Commission has made an important first step in shaping a bright future for the community college movement, enhancing the quality of college programs, and strengthening public confidence in community, technical, and junior colleges.

American Association of Community
and Junior Colleges

Larry W. Tyree
Chair
Board of Directors

Dale Parnell
President and Chief
Executive Officer

April 1988

COMMISSION ON THE FUTURE OF COMMUNITY COLLEGES

Nancy L. Kassebaum
Honorary Chairman
United States Senate

Ernest L. Boyer, Chairman
The Carnegie Foundation for
the Advancement of Teaching

Jack W. Peltason
Co-chairman, University of
California, Irvine

Harold D. Albertson
Richland College

K. Patricia Cross
Harvard University

Wilhelmina R. Delco
Texas Legislature

Nolen M. Ellison
Cuyahoga Community
College District

Paul A. Elsner
Maricopa County Community
College District

Marvin Feldman
Fashion Institute
of Technology

Alfred P. Fernandez
Ventura County Community
College District

R. Jan LeCroy
Dallas Citizens Council

Frank Newman
Education Commission
of the States

Wayne T. Newton
Kirkwood Community College

Terry O'Banion
The League for Innovation in
the Community College

David R. Pierce
Illinois Community
College Board

George E. Potter
Jackson Community College

Beverly S. Simone
Western Wisconsin
Technical College

Joyce S. Tsunoda
University of Hawaii
Community College System

James L. Wattenbarger
Institute of Higher Education,
University of Florida

EX OFFICIO

Lawrence W. Tyree
Dallas County Community
College District

David Ponitz
Sinclair Community College

Dale Parnell, American
Association of Community
and Junior Colleges

STAFF

Nancy R. Armes
Executive Director

Martha Hughes
Research Associate
Joel D. Lapin
Research Associate
Kay McClenney
Research Associate
Diana F. Rangel
Administrative Assistant
Mary Ann Roe
Ellen Sullivan
Allen A. Witt
Research Assistants

PROLOGUE

The Commission on the Future of Community Colleges undertook its charge to analyze and make recommendations concerning issues that would impact the future of community colleges with great care.

As we worked through our deliberations, several assumptions became apparent. We agreed from the very first that the Commission should organize its work and make its recommendations based on the comprehensive mission of the community college. There was the option, carefully considered, to hone in on a more focused theme. We considered, for example, concentrating exclusively on teaching and learning, which established themselves early on as major thrusts of our report. But while teaching and learning are central to all of the issues considered, we finally decided to address the mission of the community college through the more inclusive theme, *Building Communities*.

Thus, while the report is in no sense a definitive analysis of the community college, we have sought to touch on all major aspects of institutional life. And yet, as Commissioners, we clearly recognize that a college should set its own priorities for implementing recommendations within the framework we provide. Indeed, throughout our deliberations, we always were aware of the great diversity among community colleges. We have made a concerted effort to affirm those differences while, at the same time, looking for the commonalities, concentrating on those elements that touch the concerns of the majority of community colleges in the nation.

In seeking to prepare a useful document, we also sought to strike a balance between the pressures of the present and the challenges of the future. Generally, we have tried to project our analysis to the turn of the century, which was, quite frankly, about as far as we could see ahead. Our intent in this report is to build bridges to the future rather than to predict it.

At the same time, we are very much aware that many of the recommendations we present are well underway at many colleges. In attempting to point out worthy solutions, we wish to both acknowledge those who have made progress and challenge others to consider their own creative options.

Finally, as Commissioners, we assume that the work we have begun will continue beyond the issuing of this report. We are deeply committed to encouraging progress and, in the next phase, we hope colleges will be moved to action by starting with clear goals and criteria for evaluating successful work, and then by showcasing exemplary programs. We intend to find opportunities to share our findings and encourage community colleges to pursue recommendations in ways that fit the needs of each unique community.

We are confident about the future. The community colleges, which have contributed so powerfully to the economic and civic vitality of the nation, will, we are convinced, assume an even more consequential role in the nation's life in the days and years ahead. It is our hope that this report will assist in the achievement of that essential goal.

The Commission on the Future
of Community Colleges

"The term *community* should be defined
not only as a region to be served, but also
as a climate to be created."

I

The Mission: Building Communities

The network of community, technical, and junior colleges in America is unique and extraordinarily successful. It is, perhaps, the only sector of higher education that truly can be called a *movement*, one in which the members are bound together and inspired by common goals.*

From the very first, these institutions, often called "the people's colleges," have stirred an egalitarian zeal among their members. The open-door policy has been pursued with an intensity and dedication comparable to the Populist, the Civil Rights, and the Feminist crusades. While more elitist institutions may define excellence as exclusion, community colleges have sought excellence in service to the many. While traditional institutions too often have been isolated islands, community colleges have built connections beyond the campus.

The awarding of the first Associate of Arts degree at the University of Chicago in 1900, followed by the establishment of a junior college in Mexico, Missouri in 1901, and the upward extension of public high schools at Joliet, Illinois also in 1901, marked the beginnings of the community college movement. William Rainey Harper, president of the Univer-

sity of Chicago and an aggressive advocate of the junior college, saw it as a place where students who would not otherwise attend an institution of higher learning could prepare for transfer to a senior college or could "stop naturally and honorably" at the end of the sophomore year.[1]

As early as 1926, N.W. Walker, then President of the Association of Colleges and Secondary Schools in the southern states, wrote: "The rapid rise of the junior colleges is one of the arresting facts of recent educational development in America. Within the past ten years," said Walker, "the junior college idea has been worked out in actual practice as perhaps no other single idea of so vast significance has ever been...in so short a period of time."

Since the 1920s, public community colleges have dramatically expanded, far outnumbering their private counterparts. By 1960, there were about 400 public community colleges in the United States, enrolling a little over three-quarters of a million students. In the decade that followed, enrollments grew sixfold and new community colleges opened at the rate of about one a week.

Between 1965 and 1975, total enrollment at community, technical, and junior colleges grew by 240 percent. Today, these colleges enroll

---

*In this report, the term "community colleges" will often be used to refer to the network of community, technical, and junior colleges that comprise the movement.

approximately 43 percent of the nation's undergraduates and 51 percent of all first-time entering freshmen.[2]

As members of the Commission on the Future of Community Colleges, we celebrate the stunning achievements of these essential institutions. Community colleges have become the largest single sector of higher education in the United States, and we are convinced that they are responding creatively to the education needs of millions of Americans. Without the vitality of community colleges, the history of education in twentieth century America would have been enormously diminished.

In recent years, however, the growth has slowed. Community colleges now encounter ambivalence in the larger community about their role and mission, and competing priorities within the college. Many institutions are fighting for budgets and scrambling to recruit students. The inspired sense of purpose that drove their growth in the 1960s has somewhat eroded. Community colleges, more than at any other time in their history, must now define, with greater clarity and sophistication, their distinctive mission even as they reaffirm their determination to render service to their communities and the nation.

But how should the new mission be defined?

Looking back, we are reminded that the community college was first called a "junior" institution, one that fit *vertically* into the ladder of formal learning. Then came a period of *horizontal* development as the colleges expanded to provide a full range of educational services to the surrounding region. We now see opportunities for community colleges to fulfill a still larger, more compelling mandate.

Today, in local communities and across the nation, we are threatened by excessive fragmentation and division. Cultural separations and racial tensions are increasing. Families are unstable and many neighborhoods, small and large, have lost their center. Robert Bellah, co-author of *Habits of the Heart*, observed that "since World War II, the traditions of atomistic individualism have grown stronger, while the traditions of the individual in society have grown weaker. The sense of cohesive community is lost." As never before, the nation needs institutions that recognize not only the dignity of the individual but also the interests of community.

At their best, community colleges recognize and enhance the dignity and power of individuals. Students come to colleges to pursue their own goals, follow their own aptitudes, become productive, self-reliant human beings, and, with new knowledge, increase their capacity and urge to continue learning. Serving individual interests must remain a top priority of community colleges. But they can do much more. By offering quality education to all ages and social groups, community colleges can strengthen common goals as individuals are encouraged to see beyond private interests and place their own lives in larger context. Community colleges, through the building of educational and civic relationships, can help both their neighborhoods and the nation become self-renewing.

When the observant Frenchman Alexis de Tocqueville visited the United States in the

1830s, he warned that "as individualism grows, people forget their ancestors and form the habit of thinking of themselves in isolation and imagine their whole destiny is in their hands." To counter fragmentation, Tocqueville argued in *Democracy in America*, "Citizens must turn from the private inlets and occasionally take a look at something other than themselves."

We propose, therefore, that the theme "Building Communities" become the new rallying point for the community college in America. We define the term "community" not only as a region to be served, but also as a climate to be created.

Building communities is, we believe, an especially appropriate objective for the community college because it embraces the institution's comprehensive mission. But the goal is not just *outreach*. Perhaps more than any other institution, the community college also can inspire *partnerships* based upon shared values and common goals. The building of community, in its broadest and best sense, encompasses a concern for the whole, for integration and collaboration, for openness and integrity, for inclusiveness and self-renewal.

Indeed, John Gardner, in presenting the 1987 Harry S Truman Lecture to the American Association of Community and Junior Colleges, observed that "the community college can perform a convening function at which representatives of various fragments and interests come together in unofficial but serious discussion of community problems." The college can, Gardner concludes, "be an effective convener, a valuable forum, a meeting ground where the common good is discussed." In such a spirit, community colleges can, we believe, become

sources of educational, civic, and cultural renewal.

Building community must, of course, begin at home. If the college itself is not held together by a larger vision, if trustees, administrators, faculty, and students are not inspired by purposes that go beyond credits and credentials, the community college will be unable to build effective networks of collaboration beyond the campus. If the college itself is not a model community, it cannot advocate community to others.

In pursuit of this assignment, community colleges have no easy task. Most students are commuters, a vast majority have other commitments and attend part-time. There is a bringing together of young, not-so-young, and old. Many students are economically disadvantaged. The challenge is immense. What works with full-time, single, well-prepared, residential students does not necessarily work with part-time students who have jobs and families—and who have often experienced less academic success in their previous schooling.

Still, with all of the diversity, community colleges are, we believe, eager to reaffirm community on campus. While preparing this report, we found that those involved in the daily life of a college have a deep commitment to common goals, to open and candid communication, and to excellence for all. And, we believe, the community college is ready, more than at any other time in recent years, to become a still more cohesive and creative institution.

This brings us to our most essential point. At the center of building community there is teaching. Teaching is the heartbeat of the educational enterprise and, when it is successful, energy is pumped into the community, continuously renewing and revitalizing the institution. Therefore, excellence in teaching is the means by which the vitality of the college is extended and a network of intellectual enrichment and cultural understanding is built. Good teaching requires active learning in the classroom. It calls for a climate in which students are encouraged to collaborate rather than compete. Thus, building community through dedicated teaching is the vision and inspiration of this report.

We begin, then, with the conviction that the community colleges of the nation have an urgent new mandate to fulfill—the building of communities. On the following pages we explore the meaning of community in six interlocking ways. First, partnerships for learning, the students and the teachers. Second, the curriculum to be taught. Third, the community created by the classroom. Fourth, the quality of campus life. Fifth, connections beyond the college. And, finally, the leadership required by community colleges to meet successfully the challenges of the year 2000 and beyond.

II

Partnerships for Learning

STUDENTS: A NATION IN TRANSITION

In the coming century, community colleges will have, as their most essential challenge, the obligation to serve a diversity of students while affirming community at the college.

The face of America is changing. Today, slightly more than one-quarter of all white Americans are under 18 years of age, but nearly one-half of all Hispanics and over one-third of all blacks fall into this age group. Thoughtful observers warn us that our society is afflicted by growing polarization. They report that there is a strong movement toward social and economic ghettos where young blacks and Hispanics, and members of other minority groups such as Native Americans, are the most socially and economically disadvantaged.

What is especially disturbing about these trends is that black and Hispanic young people are precisely those with whom most of our nation's schools and colleges have been least successful. While 77 percent of white 18- and 19-year-olds in this country are high school graduates, only 63 percent of blacks and 50 percent of Hispanics in this age group complete secondary education.[1]

The high achievement levels attained within some segments of the growing Asian student population have been widely reported. However, it is important to note also that many Asian students—including large numbers of new immigrants—bring with them the challenges of cultural transition, economic disadvantage, and mastery of English as a second language.

Community colleges must help to solve the dropout problem. If they do not, minority students will continue to leave school at the current rate, an increasing proportion of our citizens will face the prospects of social and economic failure, and communities will languish. In the America that is emerging, the special challenge will be to overcome the social separations that restrict the quality of education and diminish prospects of civic health.

The community college has a further obligation to help students succeed in higher education. Members of minorities who complete high school are more likely than white students to attend community colleges. These colleges enroll 55 percent of all Hispanic undergraduates, 57 percent of Native American college students, 43 percent of all black students, and 42 percent of all Asian students who attend institutions of higher education in America.[2]

As a Commission, we are especially concerned about the number of students who leave college before their program has been satisfactorily completed. Equally troublesome is the fact that, because they lack basic skills, many minority students in community colleges are enrolled in remedial courses, are screened out of demanding technical programs, and are less likely to transfer. Therefore, the community college must not just enroll more minority students but also assure that they can complete successfully their courses of study.

This, then, is the central mandate. The community college must continue to offer all students an open door, and reaffirm to minority students the promise of empowerment through education. Without this opportunity, America will become a socially and economically divided nation. The spirit of community will be lost.

The demography of the nation is changing in yet another way. America is growing older, and a separation of the generations is emerging in this country. Young children are in day care centers, children are in schools, parents work away from home, and retirees have their own separate living arrangements. This generational "layering" leaves both young and old educationally and socially impoverished.

With a growing number of older students on campus, the community college has a special opportunity to build connections across the generations. The average age of students in credit classes at public community colleges is 27; when all students are counted, it is over 30. Further, 63 percent of all students enrolled in credit classes at community colleges are part-time. This is a substantial increase over the 48 percent of students enrolled part-time in 1970.

By 1992, the part-time enrollments at community colleges are expected to increase by 7 percent, the enrollment of full-time students will decline by approximately 10 percent, and perhaps as many as two-thirds of the full-time students in community colleges will have jobs.[3]

Again, because their doors are open to students regardless of age, race, or ethnic origin, the nation's community colleges can be leading architects in building new communities in America. As partners in a network of institutions stretching from coast to coast, they can help the least advantaged move into the mainstream of American life, serve students of all ages, and provide continuing education, civic empowerment, and social integration for a growing number of citizens. Such community building amidst diversity is, we believe, vital to the future of the nation.

- *The nation's community colleges should vigorously reaffirm equality of opportunity as an essential goal. Every college should declare, with pride and conviction, its determination to serve all ages and racial and ethnic groups.*

- *In pursuit of this objective, we urge that every college develop an aggressive outreach plan for disadvantaged students. Specifically, each college should create an Early Identification Program with surrounding schools, focusing first on junior high school students. The emphasis of such a program should be on counseling, on language proficiency, and on the academic preparation of students in order to increase the number of minority members who are adequately prepared for college.*

- *Community colleges also should expand and improve Outreach Programs for Adults, sponsoring projects designed to reach displaced workers, single parents, and adults who, after military service, are returning to civilian life. This traditional function will become increasingly vital by the year 2000 and beyond.*

- *We urge that community colleges give more attention to student retention. Every college should develop a comprehensive First Year Program with orientation for all full-time, part-time, and evening students. Such a program should include advising, an "early warning" system to identify at-risk students, plus career counseling and mentoring arrangements. Over the next decade, the goal should be to reduce, by 50 percent, the number of students who fail to complete the program in which they are enrolled.*

- *The community college should encourage greater intellectual and social contacts among students at the institution, seeking to bring together older and younger students and those from different ethnic and racial backgrounds so that learning for all can be enriched.*

TEACHING FACULTY: MENTORS AND SCHOLARS

Faculty are critically important in the building of a community of learning. They provide continuity to the institution. They define priorities and pass on traditions from one generation of students to another. And community colleges have, throughout the years, been extremely well served by dedicated teachers. Although college teaching is often more criticized than praised, we are impressed by how deeply faculty are committed to their tasks. They talk enthusiastically about the satisfactions of teaching and give generously of their time to students outside the classroom.

However, during our examination we found that community college faculty often feel overextended, typically teaching at least five courses per semester. Classes, especially in basic subjects, often are too large and preparation time is too short. There is, on all too many campuses, a feeling of burnout and fatigue among faculty, a loss of vitality that weakens the quality of teaching.

Further, community college faculty members, especially in career and technical programs, often do not have the support they need to keep abreast of their profession. Many feel isolated—out of touch with colleagues in their fields. We find it especially disturbing that 63 percent of the community college faculty in a national survey rated the intellectual environment at their institution as "fair" or "poor." In a climate such as this, teaching effectiveness is diminished and the potential for excellence is lost.[4]

In the days ahead, teaching will not become easier. As students become more diverse, the demands also will increase. Old patterns will no longer suffice. And great care must be taken, not just in the selection of new faculty members but also in their orientation into the college community.

We are convinced that all prospective community college teachers should communicate effectively, demonstrate the ability to use educational technology, show a commitment to the community college philosophy and the students to be served, and demonstrate qualities of leadership, as well.

Beyond excellence, which is central, the recruitment of new faculty must focus on diversity. The average full-time community college faculty member is 50 years of age. He or she has taught ten years or more. More than half the faculty are male; about 90 percent are white; less than 5 percent are black; and even fewer are Hispanic. At a time when the student body increasingly is female and black or Hispanic, community colleges can no longer live with the current arrangement. Students in such a setting, both minority and nonminority, do not have representative models or mentors.

Within the next twelve years, approximately 40 percent of all community college faculty who now teach will retire. How new faculty are selected will be one of the most important issues community colleges confront. The stakes for building community—with both diversity and professional excellence—are enormously high.

Meanwhile, we believe that the renewal of community college faculty is absolutely crucial. If renewal is not forthcoming, if faculty support is not available, the community college will have depleted its most essential resource. A report by the American Association of Community and Junior Colleges put the issue squarely:

"The staff of a college is its single greatest resource. In economic terms, the staff is the college's most significant and largest capital investment. In these terms alone, we affirm that it is only good sense that the investment should be helped to appreciate in value and not be allowed to wear itself out or slide into obsolescence by inattention or neglect."[5]

In the end, the classroom should be the greatest source of renewal for the teacher. When good teaching works, as it does every day in community colleges around the nation, the results are brilliant and enduring. Members of the faculty share ideas with colleagues and often work together on curriculum projects across the disciplines. Student progress is creatively assessed. Teachers have a shared sense of purpose. They value their roles in the teaching community. In such a setting, the teacher is renewed.

But the teaching environment in most community colleges is still more complex. Today, part-time teachers comprise about 60 percent of community college faculty, and it is estimated that about 25 percent of all community college credits are earned through classes taught by part-time teachers. The Commission is convinced that part-time faculty are not only a necessary resource but can also powerfully enrich the college through the diversity and breadth of experience they bring to the campus.

It is the conviction of the Commission, however, that the increasing numbers of part-time faculty at many colleges are a disturbing trend. Although part-time faculty members contribute to a vibrant institution, it is obviously more difficult

TABLE I

FULL- AND PART-TIME FACULTY AT COMMUNITY,
TECHNICAL, AND JUNIOR COLLEGES, 1970-1986

| Year | Full-Time | | Part-Time | |
	Number	Percent of total	Number	Percent of total
1973	89,958	59	61,989	41
1976	88,277	44	111,378	56
1980	104,777	44	134,064	56
1986	110,909	40	164,080	60

SOURCE: *Community, Technical, and Junior Colleges: A Summary of Selected National Data,* American Association of Community and Junior Colleges, 1987.

for them to advise students, to collaborate with colleagues, and to participate in institutional life in ways that build community. A healthy balance between part-time and full-time faculty is required.

For community colleges to fulfill their potential, part-time faculty, regardless of their numbers, must be carefully integrated into the institution. For these colleagues, the need for orientation and professional development is even greater. Above all, part-time faculty should meet high professional standards and be available to students. They, like all college staff, should be carefully evaluated so that high performance can be the basis for reappointment.

We conclude that faculty play a critical role in the building of community. Those who teach control the academic standards, shape the curriculum, and help create the climate for

learning on the campus. Through their professional priorities and in their relationships with students, faculty sustain or weaken the intellectual and social environment of the college.

• *We urge each community college to commit itself to the recruitment and retention of a top quality faculty and to the professional development of these colleagues. It is through the careful selection and continuous renewal of faculty that the future of the community college will be built.*

• *The percentage of faculty members who are black, Hispanic, and Asian should be increased. For this to be accomplished, future teachers should be identified from among minority students in high schools and community colleges. Such students should be assigned mentors who encourage them to consider teaching. Future teachers also should be invited to serve as peer tutors and teachers' aides.*

- *We recommend that graduate fellowships be available to minority students who plan to teach in community colleges.*

- *Every community college should have a Faculty Renewal Plan, one developed in consultation with the faculty. Such a plan should include campus workshops, faculty-led seminars, departmental and campus-wide retreats, participation in national conferences, short-term leaves, intercollegiate faculty exchanges, and sabbaticals.*

- *Further, we propose that at least 2 percent of the instructional budget at every community college be set aside for professional development.*

- *An Innovative Teachers' Fund is recommended for every college, one that would give small grants to faculty members to improve teaching.*

- *Every community college should have a policy regarding the selection, orientation, evaluation, and renewal of part-time faculty. These colleagues should be given the professional support necessary in order to be effective members of the college community.*

- *We urge that unrestrained expansion of part-time faculty be avoided. As a general rule, a majority of credits awarded by a community college should be earned in classes taught by full-time faculty. Any deviation from this goal should be based upon clearly defined institutional objectives.*

III

Curriculum: From Literacy to Lifelong Education

Throughout the years, the nation's community colleges have adjusted to the needs of students and to marketplace demands. Responding quickly and creatively to changing educational mandates is one of their unique characteristics. As new technologies are created, new certificate and degree programs are introduced. When older citizens need enrichment, community colleges provide the plans. Such responsiveness has contributed immeasurably to the economic vitality of the nation and enriched, as well, the quality of students' lives.

But responsiveness should be guided by clear goals. And we note with concern that some community colleges have added functions almost randomly, it seems. The curriculum is too fragmented, and learning, at some institutions, has become compartmentalized. Faculty work mainly within departments, administrators often are removed from instructional concerns, and students are not able to see connections or place their learning in perspective. Most disturbing is the fact that, at far too many colleges, general education has been allowed to drift. The larger meaning has been lost.

We conclude that it is through a curriculum with coherence that community also can be built. And we set forth four academic goals the nation's community colleges should vigorously pursue as we move toward the year 2000.

First, all community college students should become proficient in the written and the spoken word.

Second, all students should learn about the human heritage and the interdependent world in which they live.

Third, the community college should offer first-rate technical education and career-related programs to prepare students for working in the Information Age.

Finally, the community college should make available to adults a rich array of short term and continuing education courses to encourage lifelong learning and help students meet their social, civic, and career obligations.

LITERACY FOR ALL

All community college students must become proficient in the written and spoken word and have the ability to read with comprehension, write with clarity, and effectively speak and listen.

Computational skills are an important element of literacy, as well. Viewed from one perspective, the number system is, in fact, a universal language, and all students should become competent in its use. These skills are critical in the quest for community since it is through language that human beings interact with one another and through the shared use of symbols that traditions are sustained.

Literacy is essential both for the individual and society. To sustain community, the capacity to engage in common discourse is crucial. But literacy, at the highest level, means not just clarity of expression, it means integrity as well. In a world that concentrates more on symbols than on substance, both honesty in the shaping of ideas and courtesy in listening are crucial. Indeed, integrity in communication helps to hold communities together.

Concerns about literacy are pervasive, not only in educational institutions but throughout society. "Adult literacy" has captured the attention of many groups. Although not all the sensationalized headlines about illiteracy in this country can be supported by the facts, it is still shocking that there are citizens who cannot read simple words and that a larger group cannot conduct transactions necessary to daily life. There is an urgent need for all adults to become linguistically prepared.

In strengthening adult literacy, community colleges have a crucial role to play. They offer adults an environment of respect and have the capacity to deal with other community agencies as well. If a coordinating agency for adult literacy has not already been established, we propose that community colleges perform this important function. Several states have already enacted laws clarifying the role of the community college in this regard. In these states, the community college coordinates a literacy network, not by providing all basic skills education, but by ensuring that agencies work together to address the problem.

Commission members are particularly disturbed by the decline of good communication in the classroom. Large numbers of community college students are "at risk" precisely because they lack proficiency in English. When we met with faculty, they confirmed overwhelmingly that the basic problem was that so many students could not write clearly or read with comprehension. This was reinforced by a Carnegie Foundation survey that revealed that 75 percent of the community college faculty questioned felt that the academic ability of their students was "fair" or "poor." Seventy-two percent said that their institution spent too much time teaching students "what they should have learned in high school."

Clearly, community colleges serve and must continue to serve a large number of academically underprepared students. And they achieve important results. Pre-college developmental programs help academically deficient students, thereby increasing student retention and program completion. Effective developmental education programs ensure standards of academic excellence and help each student build the skills necessary to succeed in subsequent courses—and in the work place.

But this foundation work must be only the beginning. During college, every student—not just those with problems—should learn to write more clearly, read with greater comprehension, listen with more discrimination, speak with more precision, and, through critical thinking, develop the capacity to apply knowledge to new concepts. This calls not only for a basic course in communications skills for every student, but also for the teaching of good communication in every class.

- *All community college students should become proficient in the written and oral use of English. To help achieve this goal, community college faculty should work with teachers in surrounding schools to improve the communications skills of students.*

- *We recommend that the reading, writing, and computational ability of all first-time community college students be carefully assessed when they enroll. Those not well prepared should be placed in an intensive developmental education program. Community colleges must make a commitment, without apology, to help students overcome academic deficiencies and acquire the skills they need to become effective, independent learners.*

- *All community college students should complete a collegiate English course with emphasis on writing. Beyond this basic requirement, good oral and written communication should be taught in every class.*

- *English teachers must have time to critique carefully what students write. Specifically, we recommend that student enrollment in the basic English course be restricted to no more than 25 students. Whenever possible, colleges should consider establishing writing labs, scheduled in sufficient blocks of time so that students may receive individual tutoring.*

- *We propose that adult literacy programs, when appropriate, be coordinated as a part of the public service mandate of the community college. This important mission should be defined by statute at the state level.*

A CORE OF COMMON LEARNING

Today's college students are products of a society in which the demands of the individual boom forth on every side, while the claims of community are weak. Older students are often preoccupied with day-to-day concerns, and there is little time for reflection or for an education that can enlarge horizons. Many students come to the community college with narrow backgrounds, and, for them, career education may mean only gaining skills for a specific job. Job training is a worthy goal for an unemployed adult, but it does not open the door wide enough.

Through lack of attention to general education, community colleges often exacerbate this tendency toward narrowness. Some community colleges offer a coherent program, one in which the separate courses are directed toward larger ends. Others offer a smorgasbord of courses, and students pick and choose their way to graduation, following the so-called distribution arrangement.

We conclude that strengthening general education is one of the most urgent obligations community colleges confront. Specifically, the aim of a community college education must be not only to prepare students for productive careers, but also to take them beyond their narrow interests, broaden their perspectives, and enable them to live lives of dignity and purpose.

Each student is unique, and individual differences should be served. But all students are also members of a larger human community, and education at its best prepares students who are knowledgeable about the world in which they live. There is, we conclude, an urgent need to provide a core experience of common learning. It is important that all students be able to put their lives in historical and social perspective and be prepared to meet their social and civic obligations.

This is an awesome agenda. It calls for more than idealized statements in catalogs. The larger perspective we have in mind means more than a grab bag of unrelated courses. We are convinced that an effective general education is one that provides students a more integrated view of knowledge and a more authentic view of life. This should be the goal of every community college in the nation.

To achieve this end, we suggest a core curriculum that focuses first on language, including the written and spoken symbol systems. Mathematics, the arts, and health are core learning assignments, too. Community college students also should be introduced to their heritage, to membership in groups and institutions, to science, technology, and the environment. Such a curriculum should not only give students essential knowledge, but should also help them make connections across the disciplines. In the end, they should be able to apply their knowledge to contemporary issues.

There is a related problem that should be seriously acknowledged. While preparing this report we were forced to conclude that Americans remain shockingly ignorant about the heritage of other nations. Students cannot identify world leaders or the capitals of other countries at a time when the destinies of all nations are interlocked. While some students have a global perspective, the majority, although vaguely concerned, are inadequately informed about the interdependent world in which they live. They lack historical understanding and have little knowledge of significant social trends that will consequentially shape their lives.

The community college experience must help students see beyond the boundaries of their own narrow interests. Students living in the twenty-first century will confront daily the reality of an interdependent world. Therefore, we strongly urge that the general education sequence provide students with an understanding of cultures other than our own.

Finally, the Commission was reminded, time and time again, that in many career and technical programs there is little time for general education. The response, we believe, should be to integrate general education within the specialized studies program—through interdisciplinary courses, special seminars, and the like. The community college, more than any other higher education institution, should overcome departmental narrowness by integrating technical and career studies with the liberal arts. As students relate general and specialized education, they begin to make connections, gain perspective, and integrate knowledge. This is at the heart of community building in higher education.

- *All community college associate degree students should complete a core curriculum, one that provides historical perspective, an understanding of our social institutions, knowledge of science and technology, and an appreciation of the visual and performing arts.*

- *We urge that the core curriculum at the community college contain an international perspective, including a study of nonwestern cultures.*

- *We recommend that the core curriculum be integrated into technical and career programs so that students place their specialization in larger context and relate learning to contemporary problems.*

- *Finally, community colleges should find creative new ways by which the goals of common learning can be accomplished—through all-college seminars, film series, and symposia, for example. Nontraditional arrangements such as these can be especially important for students enrolled in nondegree or part-time programs.*

THE ESSENTIALNESS OF WORK

Education for work has been a key component of the community college mandate from the first. Early in this century L. V. Koos described work preparation as a singular contribution of the movement. The importance of preparation for work was also stressed by the 1948 Truman

Commission report on higher education. Beginning in the 1960s, career and technical programs tended to dominate the curriculum. Currently, about two-thirds of all community college students are enrolled in career and technical studies, and about 25 percent of the associate degrees awarded are in the liberal arts. The largest numbers are in engineering, business, and health.

Today, the nation's communities face loss of productivity, unemployment, and industry decline. They are in search of economic renewal. As we move toward the year 2000, the proportion of 16- to 24-year-olds in the United States will shrink by almost two million, or 8 percent. More than 80 percent of the growth in the work force will come from women and minority groups traditionally underserved by the educational system.[1] We conclude that the community college will have a pivotal role to play in rebuilding communities by responding to local economic needs, by preparing an educated work force, and by training and retraining workers and executives, as well.

Preparation for work should begin in school. All high school students, not just the college bound, should, we believe, develop the linguistic and computational skills necessary to enter the job market. Further, they should learn good work habits and, through counseling, be introduced to various career options.

Most comprehensive high schools do not have the teachers or facilities to provide a full range of solid technical education programs for students that would prepare them adequately for

TABLE II

PERCENTAGE OF ASSOCIATE DEGREES AWARDED IN
TOP-RANKING FIELDS OF STUDY, 1984-85

Field of Study	Percent of Total
MEN	
Engineering Technologies	27
Liberal Arts/General Studies	23
Business & Management	20
Other Fields	29
WOMEN	
Business & Management	32
Health Sciences	24
Liberal Arts/General Studies	23
Other Fields	21

SOURCE: *Less Than 4-Year Awards in Institutions of Higher Education*, Center for Education Statistics, U.S. Department of Education, 1987.

specified work. Collaborative programs, however, are one important answer. Dale Parnell, in his provocative work, *The Neglected Majority*, has proposed a two-plus-two tech prep/associate degree arrangement in which some students, in their last two years of high school, would begin a technical education program linked to a community college program. Over four years, as students complete the associate degree, they would develop skills and aptitudes that prepare them for the work place.

The Commission believes that associate degree technical education programs will assume more importance in the next decade. The U.S. Department of Labor estimates that 75 percent of all job classifications will require some form of postsecondary education for entry by 1995. If that figure is accurate, the associate degree

and certificate technical education programs in community colleges that prepare people for immediate entry into mid-level professional, technical, and skills positions will match future needs.

The fundamental question is, of course, what does it mean to prepare students for work in the Information Age?

We acknowledge that if technical education programs are too narrow, if work cannot be a broadening experience, then the student may achieve only short-term gain. We also acknowledge that the utility of education and the dignity of vocation have important value, not just for those enrolled in technical programs, but for those in general and transfer studies, too. Only by placing emphasis on both can all students help in the building of community.

Unfortunately, the blending of general and technical education may be thwarted by rigid articulation agreements. In most states, students who plan to transfer must complete general education courses which match those required by the senior institution. At the same time, a significant percentage of technical education credits are arbitrarily deemed not transferable by four-year colleges. Thus, the student who wants to complete a baccalaureate degree is often greatly hampered.

The Commission recommends exploring new ways to combine technical and general studies throughout the undergraduate experience. As one approach, we recommend "inverted" degree programs. Such arrangements, which permit students to specialize in the first two years and then complete their general sequence at a baccalaureate institution, have been quite successful in several states. In the inverted program, emphasis on the core curriculum—while still critically important—would begin in the community college and extend throughout the four-year sequence. By affirming both technical and liberal learning, the prospects of broadening work preparation would be enormously enhanced.

- *We urge that schools and community colleges join in 2 + 2 or 2 + 1 arrangements in which technical studies programs begun in high school are completed in a community college, either in a certificate or associate degree program.*

- *We recommend that experimental "inverted degree" models be available in every state. Through such arrangements the specialized two-year programs would be followed by a general education sequence offered by a four-year institution.*

- *Community college faculty should take the lead in closing the gap between the so-called "liberal" and "useful" arts. Students in technical studies should be helped to discover the meaning of work. They should put their special skills in historical, social, and ethical perspective. Those in traditional arts and science programs should, in turn, understand that work is the means by which we validate formal education.*

- *We recommend that every college develop a clear agreement among faculty, students, and administrators on what portions of the core curriculum are to be included in technical education programs.*

- *We also urge that special attention be given to the selection of technical education faculty and administrators to assure that they can develop up-to-date programs that integrate the core curriculum and technical education.*

- *Finally, we are convinced that the Associate of Applied Science degree will take on increasing importance in the Information Age. To insure the viability of this degree, we urge that attention be given to the communication, computational, and problem solving competence, as well as the technical education skills, of all AAS degree students.*

LEARNING FOR A LIFETIME

The community college, perhaps more than any other institution, is committed to lifelong learning. It has opened its doors to those who wish to reenter time and time again.

By the year 2000, a community college's success in building community will be measured, at least in part, by how often its students return to college, not only for refresher courses, but for new and different career preparation and life enrichment. Again, it is the conviction of the Commission that lifelong learning is an essential mission that the community college is uniquely qualified to fulfill.

Already, the power of continuing education can be seen. In 1986, almost a million continuing education courses, programs, and seminars were offered by the nation's community colleges, and more than 30,000 special projects were conducted. Noncredit enrollments equalled, and in some cases, exceeded credit enrollment.

Further, employers all across the country are discovering that it is to their advantage to form linkages with the local community college. Worker training is the central focus of this partnership. What the land-grant county agent did for the farmer a century ago, the community college is doing for the Information Age industrialist today.

We are convinced that this is only the beginning. The Department of Labor estimates that by the year 2000 a worker will change careers three times and change jobs at least seven. There will be an urgent need for retraining workers as they move from one job to another.

A recent Bureau of Labor Statistics survey found that between 1981 and 1986 more than 11 million workers were dislocated. Even though more than five million of these displaced workers had three years or more of tenure, many of their job losses were permanent.

We conclude that, for many workers, learning will be lifelong. It is unrealistic to think that young adults can be trained in skills that will serve a lifetime. And the master plan of every community college should creatively respond to its essential role of training and retraining the vital work force on which the nation's prosperity will depend.

Lifelong learning also means enrichment. People are living longer and, for many, the quality of life will be measured by the ability to stay intellectually engaged. Indeed, when adults are asked to list topics in which they have an interest, personal enrichment, general education, and public affairs rank high. The community college should be creative in responding to these interests.

But we are troubled that some so-called enrichment courses offered by community colleges are marginal in their significance—and in their quality as well. Such courses invite critics to charge that the institution is not serious about learning. Continuing education courses can be practical and helpful, of course, but they should not trivialize the meaning of collegiate study. We believe that *all* courses—whether they are offered in the day, during evenings, or on weekends—should impart knowledge, develop skills, and clarify values. They should not be only entertaining. Further, the adult education program should, perhaps more than any other part of the curriculum, be developed cooperatively with other agencies in the community. Unnecessary duplication should be avoided.

Finally, in the building of community there is the matter of the civic education of adults. If Americans are to be well-informed, education for citizenship must become a lifelong process. In a world where public policy decisions have awesome implications, creating commonwealth becomes an urgent obligation.

Community colleges also have an obligation to continue to educate society's policy shapers: journalists, corporate directors, congressional and legislative staff members, judges, senior civil servants, labor leaders, and clergy, for example. Public policy programs for these specialists can be offered in a variety of ways— through weekend seminars, special institutes, and "alumni colleges" that bring graduates back to campus for short-term courses.

Sir Eric Ashby, the British academic, has observed that the difference between educating for citizenship in the nineteenth century and today is that the nineteenth-century graduate "could assume that he would grow old in a world familiar to him as a youth." Continues Ashby: "We are living in the first era for which this assumption is false, and we have not yet faced the consequences of this fact."

Humanity has always lived with change, but the rate of change today is very great and the pace will not diminish. A major challenge is to provide learning that is lifelong. This is, we believe, a special mandate if community is to be affirmed and continuously renewed.

- *Every community college should work with employers to develop a program of recurrent education to keep the work force up-to-date and well-educated. Such a strategy should become an integral part of any regional economic development program.*

- *As a part of their basic introduction to the college, all community college students should be introduced to the vision of lifelong learning. They should be reminded that work, leisure, and education will be intertwined throughout life.*

- *Adult and continuing education programs should provide enrichment for citizens throughout their lives. Specifically, we urge that continuing education courses be a high priority, that they draw upon the intellectual and cultural resources of the college, and that they reflect both community needs and the educational traditions of the institution.*

- *Further, we propose that each community college, in developing its continuing education program, coordinate with schools, churches, and other groups to avoid unnecessary duplication.*

- *Finally, we recommend that community colleges lead the way in civic literacy for adults. Specifically, we recommend that colleges consider introducing a new civic education program for adults, one that would focus on government, public policy, and contemporary issues. The approach would be interdisciplinary, with the aim of encouraging responsible citizen participation.*

IV

The Classroom as Community

EXCELLENCE IN TEACHING

The community college should be the nation's premier teaching institution. Quality instruction should be the hallmark of the movement. Community colleges, above all others, should expect the highest performance in each class and be creative and consistent in the evaluation of results. Indeed, it is the conviction of the Commission that the theme *Building Communities* is applied most appropriately to the classroom, where both intellectual and social relationships are strengthened and where teachers and students can be active partners in the learning process.

We agree with Mortimer Adler's conclusion that "all genuine learning is active, not passive. It involves the use of the mind, not just the memory. It is a process of discovery in which the student is the main agent, not the teacher." [1] All students, not just the most aggressive or most verbal, should be actively engaged. It is unacceptable for a few students to participate in the give and take with faculty while others are allowed to be mere spectators. Since active involvement of all students is critical, more "time on task" is needed, with frequent feedback and creative interaction between students and faculty. In such a climate students also learn from one another.

According to Carl Schorske, the test of a good teacher is captured in the question, "Do you regard 'learning' as a noun or a verb? If as a noun, as a thing to be possessed and passed along, then you present your truths, neatly packaged, to your students. But if you see 'learning' as a verb!—the process is different." [2] Again, building community is essentially related to learning, and the classroom is where it must begin, precisely because it is here that students are regularly assembled.

Collaborative learning should, we believe, be strengthened. Since this is the way most consequential problems are solved, students who learn to work together are better prepared to meet life's obligations. Further, recent research suggests that collaboration in the classroom has special value for nontraditional and underprepared students. Such teaching arrangements—which are based upon high academic standards—also increase the spirit of community, as they bring the participants together and provide a common purpose.

We urge, therefore, that students be asked to participate in collaborative projects, that they work together on group assignments, that special effort be made, through small-group work within larger lecture sections, to create conditions that underscore cooperation as essential in the classroom and in society, as well.

Constraints of time often restrict the building of teaching and learning communities at the community college. Today, more than two-thirds of the students and over half of the faculty are part-time. Part-time students may take five or more years to complete an associate degree. Even full-time students have other pressing commitments. Approaches that may work for residential, full-time students who are young, well prepared, and free of responsibility often are inappropriate for commuting, part-time, adult students with work and family responsibilities.

When time constraints are coupled with large classes, problems grow more perplexing. Again, during interviews, the Commission heard faculty say they were being spread too thin—with classes too large, time too short, too many essays to grade, and too many inadequately prepared students. We understand the budget pressures, and yet excellence cannot be accomplished by cutting corners on quality instruction. Community colleges should, we believe, review carefully the matter of class size and teacher load, especially in the core general education program where essential courses are often the most crowded and in developmental sequences where individual attention is most critical.

Also, to achieve excellence in the classroom, quality instruction must be consistently rewarded. American higher education continues to draw its inspiration from the colonial college with its focus on the student, on general education, and on loyalty to the college. But higher education in this country has also been powerfully inspired by the German university, with its focus on the professoriate, on specialization, and on loyalty to the discipline more than to the college.

When The Carnegie Foundation for the Advancement of Teaching surveyed faculty nationwide, 75 percent of the community college respondents said their loyalty to their academic discipline was most important to them, while one-third felt very strong loyalty to their institution.

The Foundation also found that 70 percent of faculty were interested more in teaching than research. And among community colleges, those preferring teaching comprised over 90 percent. Further, almost 70 percent of community college faculty surveyed strongly agreed that teaching effectiveness, not publication, should be the primary criterion for recognition.

While not every community college faculty member is a publishing researcher, each should be a *dedicated scholar*—including those involved in technical and applied education. But for this to be a realistic goal, the meaning of scholarship must be broadened.

In addition to the scholarship of *discovering* knowledge, through research, it is also important to recognize the scholarship of *integrating* knowledge, through curriculum development, the scholarship of *applying* knowledge, through service, and, above all, the scholarship of *presenting* knowledge, through effective teaching. These are areas of vital importance to community colleges.

26

Finally, excellence in teaching should be honored. Salary and evaluation decisions should be based primarily on teaching effectiveness. Programs to acknowledge teaching excellence should be established at every community college.

A new strategy for the evaluation of teaching and learning is, we believe, key to quality in the community college classroom. Professor K. Patricia Cross has recently proposed that a teacher, to be most effective, must be considered a *classroom researcher*—one who is involved in the evaluation of his or her own teaching and learning, even as it takes place. Such a person should be trained to be a careful observer of the teaching process, to collect feedback on what and how well students learn, and to evaluate the effectiveness of instruction. This approach to evaluating teaching asks faculty to make a clear connection between how they teach and what students learn. It establishes the classroom as both a teaching *and* research environment, a place where pedagogical questions can be thoughtfully pursued.

- *We recommend that good teaching be the hallmark of the community college movement. Students should be active, not passive, learners. The classroom should be a place where ideas are vigorously pursued and cooperative learning is encouraged.*

- *We urge that class size in core curriculum and developmental study courses be restricted, and that all members of the faculty be encouraged to teach in the core academic program and strengthen the literacy skills of their students.*

- *Distinguished Teaching Chairs or other appropriate recognitions should be established at every college. Such arrangements would honor excellent teaching and provide salary increases as well as support for professional growth activities.*

- *Community colleges should define the role of the faculty member as classroom researcher—focusing evaluation on instruction and making a clear connection between what the teacher teaches and how students learn.*

TECHNOLOGY AND TEACHING

In community colleges, technology is an important tool for teaching and for learning. Television extends the classroom electronically far beyond the campus. At colleges from coast to coast, students can, through on-line terminals, gain access to library resources, and the word processor extends the creative power of faculty and students.

As we look to the twenty-first century, the challenge of technology in support of teaching will grow even more intense. Technology, if well used, can democratize the learning environment. Through technology, all students, regardless of their backgrounds, can travel to the moon or travel to the bottom of the ocean. Through technology, every college can provide a nine million volume library for its students. With programmed learning, students can learn at different rates.

The effective use of technology increases retention. Through technology, college officials can keep better track of who their students are, what they need, and how they are progressing. The system can flag a student who is absent or who is performing unsatisfactorily. Within the classroom, in learning labs, and in tutoring sessions, new interactive computers make drill and practice much easier for the student. By increasing feedback, they expand faculty ability to improve learning. Appropriately used, technology can increase the quality of human interaction. It can, for example, handle more of the routine and thus open up time for discussion.

Finally, technology should surely encourage innovation. Electronic teaching may provide effective exchanges of information, ideas, and experiences. New technologies promise to enrich the study of literature, science, mathematics, and the arts through words, pictures, and auditory messages. But televisions, calculators, word processors, and computers cannot make value judgments. They cannot teach students wisdom. That is the mission of the faculty, and the classroom must be a place where the switches are sometimes turned off. To achieve this goal, the support of technology must be linked to college objectives.

The goal should be to use technology as a means, not an end. And the challenge for the community college will be to build a partnership between traditional and nontraditional education, letting each do what it can do best. If technology is not made evenly available to all students—if some colleges leap ahead while others lag behind—the gap between the haves and have nots in education will increase.

Thus, we conclude that each community college should make clear the assumptions on which its use of technology is based, and there should be a plan that precedes the hardware and is regularly updated. Most important, faculty must be involved both in establishing priorities and developing the mechanisms to support these priorities.

- *We recommend that every community college develop a campus-wide plan for the use of technology, one in which educational and administrative applications can be integrated.*

- *We also propose incentive programs for faculty who wish to adapt educational technology to classroom needs.*

- *Further, we recommend that a clearinghouse be established at the American Association of Community and Junior Colleges to identify educational software of special value to the community college.*

- *The community college—through technology—should continue to extend the campus, providing instruction to the work place and to schools, and scheduling regional teleconferences for community forums in continuing education.*

- *Finally, we recommend that new uses of technology be explored. Specifically, community colleges should lead the way in creating electronic networks for learning, satellite classrooms, and conferences that connect colleges from coast to coast, creating a national community of educators who transcend regionalism on consequential issues.*

V

The College as Community

A VISION SHARED

Thus far, we have considered the building of community primarily through formal education in the classroom. But there remains a basic question to be asked. Can there be community *beyond* the classroom?

Looking to the year 2000, the community college increasingly will be a place where students of all ages will come and go, often in the evening, wedging college in between other pressing duties. In such a setting, is it realistic to consider the college as something more than a network of unconnected classrooms, a place in which the whole is greater than the sum of its parts? The Commission struggled with this question, determining it to be among the most challenging facing community colleges.

The sentimental tradition of the college campus as a tranquil island where students and faculty spend their days together in a monastic setting never did fit the community college. This idealized view of college learning will be even less relevant in the years ahead.

Still, it is our conclusion that a community college, even with diversity, can be inspired by a larger vision. Indeed, Paul Elsner, Chancellor of the Maricopa County Community College District, has written powerfully about the possibility that community colleges have begun to lose their vitality precisely because there is no vision widely shared. At many institutions, the sense of community is virtually absent as part-time students move in and out as faculty "live on the margins," to borrow Burton Clark's image from_ The Academic Life. Elsner insists that the community college should assume greater responsibility for maintaining a community, by which he means the meeting ground on which issues of effective teaching and learning are discussed and, hopefully, reaffirmed.

Community college professionals are remarkably resilient. More than 90 percent responding to the Carnegie survey agreed that their college was a "good place" or "fairly good place" for them to be. But to experience the college-wide community as a source of renewal, they need more opportunities to relate to one another.

We found, for example, that there is often little connection between instructional programs and student services on the campus. On many campuses, subgroups, departments, and small enclaves of learners provide the only meaningful contact. Often there are sharp divisions between part-time and full-time students, and even more frequent is the separation between day and evening students and programs. A community college can be a very lonely place for many evening attendees who often are not considered "the real students."

What students do at the counselor's office, in the registration line, the cafeteria, the library, and the business office all combine to influence the outcome of their college education. The challenge in the building of community is to extend the resources for learning college-wide and to see academic and nonacademic life as interlocked.

There is a related issue that adds urgency to the agenda. In society at large and even, we fear, in higher education, we sense a growing climate of distrust, sometimes hostility, among the various races and ethnic groups, and even between the older and the young. In our cities, racial incidents have flared and, on campus, students from different backgrounds often isolate themselves from one another.

We are deeply troubled by this separation. A sense of wholeness is urgently required, wholeness that engenders not suspicion but community. The college cannot remain idle while students separate themselves from one another, or, worse, reinforce stereotypes and prejudices. The goal must be to build alliances between the classroom and campus life, to find group activities, traditions, and common values to be shared.

We do not suggest a residential, four-year college model. For the community college, more creative ways must be found to extend the discourse, build relationships, and stir a spirit of shared goals. Community colleges can have effective orientation sessions, all-college convocations, and other events that bring the students and the community together. Further, the community college has a special obligation to have business and counseling offices open in the evening and on weekends to serve students.

Special attention also should be given to increasing the commitment of all staff to the college—such commitment will be felt by students at every point of contact. What we seek is a climate in which the social and the intellectual relationships are strengthened, one in which the classroom is extended. Properly conceived, the community should renew itself on every occasion when there is an interaction between the student and the college.

We are convinced that if a true community of learning is to be sustained, the curricular and co-curricular activities must be joined. What we urgently need in community colleges today are *scholar/citizens*, people who are committed to the building of community—not just in the classroom, but in the financial aid office, the committee room, and the coffee shop, as well.

- *The community college should be committed to the building of community beyond the classroom. All students should be introduced to the traditions of the institution at orientation and also through lectures, cultural events, and special celebrations. The traditions of the college as a community of learning should be strengthened.*

- *Community colleges should make a full range of support services available to all students, including on weekends and evenings. Further, special efforts should be made to integrate part-time students into the educational programs of the college outside the classroom.*

- *We strongly recommend that faculty and counselors work in close collaboration. We also believe that nonfaculty personnel play a strategic role in the building of community on campus. Since their relationship with students is crucial, we urge that these colleagues be involved in discussions about college goals and priorities.*

- *Finally, the community college has a special obligation to break down separation based on age, race, or ethnic background. Specifically, we urge that younger and older students be encouraged to collaborate and establish social and intellectual relationships.*

COMMUNITY: A PERSPECTIVE THAT IS GLOBAL

In the past half-century, our planet has become vastly more crowded, more interdependent, and more unstable. Since man orbited into space, it has become dramatically apparent that we are all custodians of a single planet. The world may not yet be a global village, but surely our sense of neighborhood must expand. If students do not see beyond themselves and better understand their place in our complex world, their capacity to live responsibly will be dangerously diminished.

When drought ravages the Sahara, when war in Indochina creates refugees, neither our compassion nor our analytic intelligence can be bounded by a dotted line on a political map. We

are beginning to understand that hunger and human rights affect alliances as decisively as weapons and treaties. Dwarfing all other concerns, the mushroom cloud hangs ominously over our world consciousness. These realities and the obligations they impose must be understood by every student.

Over the past two decades, the United States' economy has become dependent on the world economy. The share of Gross National Product devoted to exports has doubled, as more and more U.S. producers have come to depend on foreign markets. Increasingly, American businesses operate on a global basis. If the college's technical programs do not take into account these global relationships so important to industry, students' skills will become obsolete.

Community colleges have, historically, been geographically restricted. They consider their "service area" to be limited to the county or district sponsoring the institution. However, these barriers are breaking down. Some community colleges now have large migrations of foreign students in their region, including large numbers of Asian and other nonwestern students. Others have been actively involved in encouraging travel abroad and even in starting campuses or programs overseas. In addition, many of the industries served by the community college have international connections.

The Commission concludes that community colleges have an urgent obligation to keep students informed about people and cultures other than their own, and that the building of partnerships must be not only local and national, but global, too. In the century ahead, parochialism is not an option.

- *We recommend that each community college coordinate—perhaps in a single office—its international activities. The goal should be to increase international awareness on campus and in the surrounding community, not only through the general education curriculum, but also through lectures, business seminars, and, when appropriate, international exchanges.*

- *We also suggest that foreign students be used as campus resources for information about the language, culture, and religions of their country so their knowledge and perspective can enrich campus life.*

SERVICE: REACHING OUT

In the building of the community college there is an opportunity and an obligation to connect the classroom to the realities of life. During our study, we saw exciting examples of service projects in which students related the theory of instruction to contemporary issues. We also found service programs rooted in the conviction that education at its best concerns itself with the humane application of knowledge to life. We conclude that this vision of service is consistent with the community college tradition and is directly linked to the building of community as well.

Service is concerned with helping others, but it is also concerned with improved learning. It is about helping students understand the value of the curriculum and discovering, in the end, that

formal learning must be considered useful, not just economically but socially as well. The larger goal is the recognition that altruism can best be appreciated as an experience rather than an abstraction.

A service program, as we envision it, adds special dimensions to the preparation for a career. Nursing students may take blood pressure at a local health fair or contribute time in a neighborhood clinic. Students training to become police officers may tutor juvenile offenders or help teach a drug education course at a community center.

Just as often, these programs are not clearly tied to a career choice, but they enhance the human skills necessary to be successful in work. Students may supervise children in a playground without planning to be physical education teachers or coaches, they may stuff envelopes for a charity mailing without planning to work in an office, and the list goes on. What is important is that these students derive profound satisfaction from their direct contacts with those who benefit from their help, and from knowing they are participating in something worthwhile. These values are important in life whether one's service is ultimately related to a career choice.

Service is not just giving out, it is also gaining insights. There will be joy and satisfaction, and pain and frustration, too. Further, if students are to be educationally influenced by a community service project, they should be asked to comment on their experience and discuss with others the lessons they have learned. In all of this, the goal is to help students consider the connection between what they learn and how they live.

- *We urge that all community colleges encourage a service program at their institution, one that begins with clearly stated educational objectives.*

- *We further recommend that students participating in service programs be asked to write about their experience and to explore with a mentor and fellow students how it is related to what they have been studying in the classroom.*

VI

Connections Beyond the College

Throughout this report we have suggested that the community college, through collaboration, can reaffirm its mandate to respond to local needs. These colleges, close to the people, can offer a convenient forum for thoughtful discourse; they can serve as a gathering place where persons of various constituencies can meet to explore common problems—whether local or global.

The community college, at its best, can be a center for problem-solving in adult illiteracy or the education of the disabled. It can be a center for leadership training, too. It can also be the place where education and business leaders meet to talk about the problems of displaced workers. It can bring together agencies to strengthen services for minorities, working women, single parent heads of households, and unwed teenage parents. It can coordinate efforts to provide day care, transportation, and financial aid. The community college can take the lead in long-range planning for community development. And it can serve as the focal point for improving the quality of life in the inner city.

We are convinced that, as we move toward the year 2000, strengthening connections beyond the college—with schools, industry, business, social agencies, and policy groups—will become a key strategy in the building of community.

PARTNERSHIPS WITH SCHOOLS

In 1884, the Massachusetts Classical and High School Teachers' Association unanimously passed a resolution that deplored the lack of cooperation between high schools and colleges. Members invited nineteen New England college presidents to meet with them, and at this first high school/college conclave a national panel called "The Committee of Ten" was established. In 1894, President Eliot of Harvard commented that "The Committee's greatest promise of usefulness" lay in its "obvious tendency to promote cooperation among school and college teachers" to advance "comprehensive education reforms."

Today, schools in America are in serious trouble. Once again, higher education has a responsibility to help solve the crisis it has, through inadvertence, perhaps helped create. We cannot have quality in our colleges if, during twelve years of public education, the teaching is inadequate and the curriculum lacks coherence.

From their inception, community colleges have been closely aligned to the nation's public schools. William Rainey Harper officially launched the community college movement by carefully strengthening the institution as a bridge between public schools and senior colleges. Harper predicted that at least 40 percent of those finishing four years of high school would want to continue further to the end of the sophomore year of college. He and others proposed that these "junior" colleges would extend the democratizing process public schools had begun. The intent was always that the two institutions would be carefully aligned.

Today, that close relationship continues. Rebuilding public schools is an urgent obligation confronting the nation, and the community college has, we believe, a crucial role to play. These institutions continue to be close to schools, they work with many of the same students, and community colleges share with schools a special relationship based on the priority that each assigns to teaching. Education is, or should be, a seamless web, and as we move toward the year 2000, school/community college partnerships should be strengthened.

- *We recommend that every community organize a school/college consortium in its region. This partnership should develop a plan for educational excellence. Such a plan would include teacher/faculty enrichment and would provide curriculum continuity in general and technical studies.*

- *We urge that community colleges work with surrounding schools to identify at-risk youth and, beginning in junior high school, provide enrichment programs that would make it possible for such students to complete high school and move on to higher education.*

- *We further recommend that community colleges report back to the high schools in their*

region regarding the academic performance of their students.

PARTNERSHIPS WITH SENIOR COLLEGES

Since the origins of the community college movement, transfer has been a primary mission. But, in recent years, transfer programs have not worked as well as is necessary. This is especially true for black and Hispanic students. We conclude that the community college has a special obligation to strengthen the transfer function for all students.

Recent Bureau of the Census data compare the earnings of adults with different educational credentials and provide a rare national insight into the incomes of associate degree recipients. The data substantiate what has long been taken for granted: the higher the academic credential, the higher the average income. Overall, associate degree recipients earn 29 percent more than high school graduates who do not continue their education. In comparison to individuals who complete some post-secondary education without earning a credential, associate degree graduates earn 15 percent more.[1]

It is also true that those earning baccalaureate degrees are still better positioned economically. We do not suggest, however, that all community college students should go on to a senior institution. Nor do we suggest that successful transfer should be defined only in terms of completing the associate degree. Students who attend a community college to get a convenient, relatively inexpensive start on a baccalaureate degree must also be well served. What we do suggest is that the transfer option should be available to all students and that the transfer pattern should be expanding not receding.

Many community college students plan to transfer. In a recent national survey of community college students, The Center for the Study of Community Colleges asked respondents this question: "What is your primary reason for enrolling at this college at this time?" Thirty-six percent indicated "preparation for transfer to a four-year college or university" to be their choice, compared to 34 percent whose goal was "to acquire skills needed for a new occupation."[2]

Goals vary, of course, by the age of students and by the curriculum they choose. For example, 56 percent of the respondents who were 20 or younger said they "planned to transfer" compared to only 16 percent of the students who were 33 or older. As for curriculum, 50 percent of all students in liberal arts classes planned to transfer, compared to only 24 percent of students in applied arts courses such as business, engineering technology, secretarial science, allied health, or criminal justice.

The Commission concludes that the transfer function must be strengthened for all students. And special emphasis must be placed on minority students' transfer needs. This will require overcoming four-year college barriers that deny credit transfer and discourage students. In many places it remains difficult to negotiate articulation and transfer arrangements on a campus by campus basis. Higher education can no longer tolerate the confusing way transcripts are interpreted. There is no justification for refusing to give academic credit for

equivalent work or for arbitrarily assigning "elective" status to course work completed in career and technical programs. These "Catch 22" arrangements violate the rights of students and bring discredit to the system.

Both interinstitutional and statewide agreements have been used to create successful transfer arrangements. Although there are constraints inherent in each of these approaches, they can, when carefully conceived, provide workable solutions which serve students.

But more must be done. At present, only 25 states have uniform articulation and transfer policies. And most of these arrangements were reached a decade or more ago. Further, most transfer policies focus either on the completion of a general education core or an associate degree. Only a few agreements clarify transfer arrangements for students who have not completed an associate degree. Clearly, there is an urgent need to develop more coherent guidelines to serve the large number of students who expect and deserve to continue their education. In building transfer arrangements, the most basic formula for success starts with faculty from the various segments of higher education talking to one another.

- *We urgently recommend that the transfer function of the community college be strengthened. Specifically, we propose that more students be urged to consider a baccalaureate degree program and be counseled to select the courses that would prepare them for such study.*

- *We also urge that special commitment be given to increasing the transfer rates among black and Hispanic students. The transfer rate among minority students should be no less than it is for students among the majority population.*

- *Coherent two-year/four-year transfer arrangements should exist in every state. Such policies should include the coordination of academic calendars and common course numbering in general education sequences.*

ALLIANCES WITH EMPLOYERS

There exists in our nation a mismatch between poorly or narrowly skilled workers and present and future work place requirements. If they are to be gainfully employed over time, workers need to become lifelong learners with the skills and intellectual tools to promote growth. It is discouraging that more and more unskilled workers are dropping out of schools or losing jobs because they cannot keep up.

In recent years the proportion of professional and technical workers in the work force has increased from 9 to 16 percent, and the proportion of managers and administrators has grown from 9 to 11 percent. This trend toward more specialized work seems to be accelerating. Employment in the five principal occupations associated with the computer field grew from 765,000 in 1970 to 1,158,000 in 1978—two and one-half times the overall growth rate in the nation's work force. At the same time, the percentage of blue collar workers decreased from 37 to 33, while farm workers, as a proportion of the labor force, plummeted from 12 to 3

percent. Only in one category—service workers—has there been an increase in the jobs in the work force for which post-high school education might not initially be required.

Obviously, more education of a different kind will be needed if a new generation of Americans is to become productively employed and find satisfaction in a world dominated by new, complicated tools. These more sophisticated work force needs, set against a backdrop of declining national productivity, make human resource development key to economic growth.

Over the past decade, many community colleges have assumed leadership in establishing collaborations with employers that make development of human resources possible. To sustain such partnerships, the community college needs to cultivate exchanges between faculty and the business world and promote the international dimensions of their programs to serve in a global economy. In the end, each partner in the effort should benefit from the collaboration—by keeping staff current and upgrading facilities and equipment at the college, and by bringing vitality to the local industry or business.

The collaborations with employers—industries, businesses, public employers, and organized labor groups—for the training of the work force and the economic development of the community are among the most important recent developments in the community college movement. They make it possible for citizens of all ages to cope with a rapidly changing, highly technological world of work and for employers to survive in an increasingly competitive environment.

- *Decision-makers across the country should fully use the resources of community, technical, and junior colleges to promote economic development efforts within their state or region.*

- *We recommend that regional clearinghouses be established to keep track of emerging work force needs in areas served by the community college. Such centers should take inventory to determine future work place patterns and describe the educational resources available at surrounding educational institutions.*

- *We propose that exchanges between educators and employers be increased to provide continuing education opportunities for faculty, to keep them current and closely related to work force demands. A long-range partnership plan with strong mutual benefits should be developed to sustain these relationships.*

- *Partnerships with employers for the training and retraining of the community's work force must be recognized as an important component of the continuing education program in community colleges.*

- *We urge that alliances with employers be carefully integrated into existing community college programs and interests. The educational and civic significance of such partnerships must be defined and continuously sustained.*

VII

Leadership for a New Century

THOSE WHO LEAD

John Gardner recently has written that:

> In some measure, what we think of as a failure of leadership on the contemporary scene may be traceable to a breakdown in the sense of community....The task of rebuilding community is not one of uncritical reaffirmation; it is a task of renewal. The process of renewal encompasses both continuity and change, building a better future on an acknowledged heritage.[1]

Building communities requires creative leaders, and the president is key. The president must move the college beyond day-to-day operations. He or she must call upon the community of learning to affirm tradition, respond to challenges, and create inspiring visions for the future. To do this, the president must be able to collaborate, bring together various constituencies, build consensus, and encourage others within the college community to lead as well.

The role of the president has, in recent years, become more complicated and more risky. There are many constituencies to serve. Generating community support takes time. Resources are often more scarce and bureaucratic encumbrances more numerous at all levels. To counter these difficulties, the president needs a passion for the job, support groups within and outside the institution, and positive recognition from beyond the college.

Looking to the year 2000, we conclude that community college presidents increasingly will need to be coalition builders. They will need strong management skills, but they will also need to inspire others. Community college leaders need vision imbued with a larger sense of educational purpose and guided by clear educational priorities for the institution. Above all else, through their vision and actions, community college leaders must affirm the centrality of teaching and continuously strengthen the college as a community of learning.

At too many community colleges we found a division between the faculty and administration. A Carnegie Foundation survey revealed that over 60 percent of community college faculty rated their administrators "fair or poor," and 66 percent said the administration at their institution is "autocratic." There is an urgent need to create new decision-making arrangements, to build trust, and to strengthen community on campus. It is our conviction that, if a spirit of community is to be built, the relationship between faculty and the president must be strong.

A word regarding the training of presidents. Since a doctorate is fairly standard, both the quality and availability of these programs becomes critical. At present, there is renewed interest among universities in supporting community college leadership programs. The Commission endorses this trend and encourages graduate schools to build creative programs to prepare community college leaders. We also urge that such programs include strong field-based components and residential requirements, and, in particular, give special attention to the educational dimensions of leadership.

In spite of recent gains, there is also a clear and pressing need to increase diversity among community college leadership. Currently, 10 percent of community college chief executive officers are women (121 of 1,222), as are 35 percent of all administrators. There are 37 black, 32 Hispanic, and 8 Asian chief executive officers in the nation's community colleges. Blacks and Hispanics are underrepresented among all administrative and faculty groups. If the community college is to enlarge leadership from among underrepresented groups, intensive recruitment of women and members of minorities as well as careful mentoring of the new recruits must become long-term strategies. The Institute for Leadership Development jointly sponsored by AAWCJC, The League for Innovation in the Community College, and Maricopa Community Colleges has been a model program for increasing representation of these groups among community college leaders. We commend and encourage such efforts.

- *In the building of community, strong presidential leadership is required. Com-munity college presidents must not only be effective day-to-day administrators, but also leaders inspired by and able to convey a larger educational vision.*

- *Looking to the year 2000, we recommend that community colleges collaborate with universities to develop creative programs aimed at preparing a new generation of community college presidents. A special effort should be made to recruit leaders from among minority and female populations.*

- *We also recommend that the president be the foremost advocate for teaching and learning at the college. It is important for all college leaders, but especially presidents, to stress the educational dimensions of the task.*

NEW MODELS OF GOVERNANCE

Presidents cannot do the job alone. If community is to be built, faculty and administrators must have similar skills. They need to move beyond normal departmental structures and focus on larger and more comprehensive matters. They should care about teaching across the curriculum. As educational leaders, members of the faculty should be aggressive advocates of excellence and innovation, both among their colleagues and in national forums.

Many more faculty and administrators need to develop their ability to lead in these ways. And many more colleges need to demonstrate their clear commitment to provide for leadership development. If we are to offer new models of governance, more than a handful of leaders are required who will look beyond the needs of an individual or group to the needs of the whole.

The organization of a faculty union, viewed on some campuses as the only means of providing adequate salaries and fair practices, can fit this broader vision, although it clearly moves away from the traditional governance function in American higher education. In collective bargaining situations, there is a major challenge shared by faculty and administrators to ensure that the college community as a whole is not harmed. The likelihood of negative impact can be diminished, however, if faculty members themselves are actively involved in collective bargaining, if negotiations are limited to salary and fair practice issues, and if faculty senates and similar bodies continue to deal with the full range of educational and administrative matters that fall within their traditional areas of concern.

What we propose, in short, is a broad-based governance design, ranging from the most formal to the most informal, to handle the full range of issues to be considered. If a college has collective bargaining, for example, it also needs a faculty senate and short-term committees, as well as conversations in the corridors to handle less formal day-to-day decisions. A community college, more than any other institution in higher education, needs flexibility. It needs to make pressing decisions quickly and to respond to changing mandates both on and off the campus.

The Commission also supports the notion that campus decisions should be made as close to the point of action as is possible and that those significantly affected by decisions should be

actively involved in the process. We believe that leaders are needed at all levels of the organization and that leadership development should be stressed, not only for the president but among faculty and mid-level administrators as well.

- *We recommend that community college governance be strengthened and that its fundamental purpose be to renew the community as a whole. Specifically, we urge that a wide range of decision-making arrangements be available on campus. These may include collective bargaining, a faculty senate, and an effective committee structure.*

- *Faculty leaders should participate actively in governance and be recognized for their work. We urge that substantive leadership development experiences be available for faculty and administrators at each community college.*

THE GOVERNING BOARD

The board of trustees helps build community as well. As a group, trustees are surrogates for a larger constituency. Their assignment is to keep the institution enlightened and more responsive. Trustees also have an obligation to represent college interests to constituents beyond the campus. If board members become merely an extension of special interests, then the college, as a community of learning, will be undercut. For this reason, the Commission strongly endorses lay trusteeship that stresses public service, with members who speak for the community as a whole.

A strong board of trustees does not involve itself in day-to-day operations. Rather, it takes the long view and seeks to sustain a proper relationship between policy and function. In publicly-funded community colleges, ones with a significant portion of this support generated locally, it is tempting for boards to focus on short-term goals, efficiency indicators, and line item control of operations. But educational leadership requires vision, not meddling. It is concerned with educational effectiveness, not just efficiency.

We conclude that if trustees are to fulfill their larger mission, they must learn about higher education, about academic traditions, and about the community college mandate. It is the legal and moral obligation of the board to preserve the rich heritage of trusteeship in America. It is significant, we believe, that 15 to 20 percent of community college trustees are new to their positions each year. Clearly, one of the most important responsibilities community colleges must assume is to educate new trustees.

There is one further governance issue. The Commission is deeply troubled by the effort on some campuses to mix internal campus decision-making with the responsibilities of trustees. This strategy replaces trustees who represent interests of the external leadership in a community with campus delegates who use the board as a forum to engage in campus debates. This blurring of governance authority weakens the system of shared decision-making in community colleges. If trustees are seen simply as another campus voice, it is difficult to protect the campus from unwarranted outside intervention. We conclude that the role of trustees and the role of internal campus governance cannot be confused if the integrity of the community college is to be retained.

- *We recommend that the role of community college trustees be strengthened. Specifically, the governing board should focus on selecting an effective leader and defining institutional goals. The board also should receive, periodically, sufficient information to know that the college's goals are being met. Trustees should not try to manage the institution.*

- *The education of community college trustees should be expanded. We strongly urge that new trustees participate in an orientation program as a condition of assuming office. We also recommend that they participate in continuing trustee education at local, regional, and national meetings.*

- *The role of the board of trustees and that of the internal governance functions should not be confused. Since trustees are the ultimate authority to which the college is accountable we recommend that faculty, staff, and student representatives not be appointed or elected to such boards as voting members.*

PROVIDING RESOURCES

Today, community college revenues are derived mainly from local and state governments and from student tuition and fees. In 1986, state appropriations accounted for almost half (48 percent) of the revenues received by community colleges; local government funding accounted for 23 percent; tuition accounted for 16 percent; and federal funds accounted for 7 percent.[2]

There are, however, great variations by state. The proportion of revenues provided by state funds ranges from 81 percent in Nevada to 25 percent in Kansas; the median is 63 percent. The proportion of revenues derived from local government ranges from 59 percent in Kansas to less than 1 percent in Kentucky; in 15 states, community colleges receive no local government funds at all. Tuition as a percentage of revenues ranges from 43 percent in Vermont to 4 percent in California.[3]

During 1986-87, the average tuition at a public community college was $687, up from $635 in 1985-86. But, again, annual tuition charges vary greatly by state, ranging from $100 in California to $1,758 in Vermont. In terms of expenditures per full-time equivalent student, community colleges devote more than half of their resources (61 percent) to instruction, to academic support services including libraries, and to student services. This compares to 42 percent at four-year colleges and 38 percent at universities.

After adjusting for inflation, current fund expenditures per full-time equivalent student at community colleges increased by only 2 percent between 1970-71 and 1984-85. In contrast, expenditures per FTE student at four-year colleges increased by 15 percent.[4]

A *Los Angeles Times* editorial recently observed:

> Community colleges need enough money to act on the quality of faculty members and on academic help to increase the number of students qualified to transfer to four-year campuses,

and to better train students who use the colleges to learn job skills. As things stand, the colleges get barely enough money to react to changes that threaten to overwhelm them.

Community colleges are increasingly the entry point to higher education for immigrants and minorities as well as a training ground for the employees whom California businesses will need in an increasingly competitive economy. They must not remain the system's stepchild.

The Commission believes community colleges have demonstrated themselves to be good stewards of the public dollar. In spite of this, in too many states, community colleges receive the state's budget leftovers, and leftovers do little to help a long undernourished system. The nation surely will pay a price for such neglect. We are convinced that the role of community colleges in revitalizing America must be vigorously reaffirmed in the local community, the state, and the nation. These colleges must receive their fair share of support at all levels.

- *We recommend that public financing of community colleges be strengthened and that states reexamine funding guidelines for these institutions. Specifically, state funding formulas should fully acknowledge the nature of services provided to part-time students and the level of support required to serve underprepared students.*

- *Corporations, private foundations, and philanthropies must be urged to remove*

TABLE III

EXPENDITURES PER FTE STUDENT AT COMMUNITY, TECHNICAL, AND JUNIOR COLLEGES, 1983-84

Purpose	Expenditure per FTE Student	Percent of Total
Instruction	$1,663	46
Institutional Support	519	14
Plant Operation/Maintenance	415	11
Student Services	304	8
Academic Support and Library Services	272	7
Auxiliary Enterprises	274	7
Other	190	5
Total	3,637	99

SOURCE: *Digest of Education Statistics*, Center for Education Statistics, U.S. Department of Education, 1987.

policies that restrict or prohibit giving to community colleges.

• *Business and industry should be encouraged to help underwrite start-up costs of technical programs in emerging and fast-changing technologies.*

ASSESSING THE OUTCOMES

A crucial task of leadership is evaluation. The key questions to be asked are these: Are the objectives of the college being met? What can be done to improve student outcomes and the effectiveness of the institution?

We have already suggested that evaluation begins in the classroom, that it must be tied to teaching and learning. Still, while classroom assessment provides information regarding student achievement in discrete courses, a college also may wish to evaluate periodically the impact of its program overall. Such

college-wide assessment should extend classroom evaluation, not replace it.

Too often, the effectiveness of community college education has been evaluated almost exclusively in terms of the number of associate degrees granted and the number of students transferring to four-year colleges and universities. While these statistics are certainly important, they do not adequately describe the diversity of student goals or the variety of desirable outcomes produced through the community college experience.

Further, assessment procedures should be shaped by the institution itself and faculty participation is absolutely crucial. State expectations obviously must be carefully considered; but a community college, tied to a local community and a unique student population, should shape the elements of its own evaluation.

But where do we begin?

The assessment of learning in community colleges should be tied to the college goals. The components of an overall assessment plan should include achievement in general education and competency in the area of specialization.

Above all, the community college should help students achieve proficiency in written and oral language. The assessment of these abilities should occur in every class and throughout the whole of the community college experience. Prior to graduation, students' proficiency in language may also be evaluated through oral and written exit examinations.

Some community colleges are using nationally normed examinations to assess the "general knowledge" of their students. Though there may be benefits in the use of standardized examinations, community college faculty should scrutinize instruments closely to determine whether they are consistent with the learning outcomes students are expected to achieve and the curriculum as taught. Assessment of higher order cognitive skills, often a weakness of standardized tests, should also be a concern.

Standardized examinations for assessing student achievement in the area of specialization are also available. Colleges may want to introduce an evaluation seminar, in the semester prior to graduation, that would include written tests, capstone projects, institutional surveys, and counseling to help students make the transition to a baccalaureate institution or to work. In addition, follow-up studies of employers and graduates should be conducted to ensure that competencies have been attained and are applicable to the work setting. However the assessment is designed, students should be reminded that the truly educated person makes connections across the disciplines and ultimately relates what he or she has learned to life beyond the campus.

Finally, if community colleges are to preserve both access and excellence, great caution must be exercised to ensure that "outcomes assessment" and "accountability" do not become code words for a new elitism. For the nation's open door colleges, quality must not be defined in terms of how many students are excluded. For the community college, quality must be measured by meeting students where they are, by good teaching, and by providing the support services students need to fulfill their academic, career, and personal objectives.

- *We urge that classroom evaluation be the central assessment activity of the community college. That process should be strengthened through faculty development programs which focus on the use of classroom evaluation to improve teaching.*

- *We recommend that each community college develop a campus-wide assessment of institutional effectiveness. Such a program should include a periodic reexamination of mission and goals, specific programs, individual student outcomes, retention rates, and the performance of graduates.*

- *Faculty and administrators in each community college should be involved in defining in explicit terms the educational outcomes which the institution aspires to produce for its students. Those outcomes should be clearly related to the mission of the college and to an informed understanding of the educational needs and goals of the college's student population.*

- *College-wide assessment processes should be designed to ascertain the extent to which desired outcomes are achieved in a student's literacy skills, general education, and area of specialization. Care should be exercised in the selection and use of standardized tests. Innovation and creativity should be encouraged in collaborative faculty efforts to devise appropriate new assessment procedures, perhaps including locally-developed examinations, student projects, performances, portfolios, oral presentations, and so on.*

- *Every college should consider further evaluation of the impact of its programs by conducting periodic interviews or surveys of current students, graduates, and employers of graduates.*

EPILOGUE

One point emerges with stark clarity from all we have said: Community colleges and the nation's future are inextricably interlocked. At a time when society's values are shaped and revised by the fashion of the marketplace, the influence of the community college must grow outward from a core of integrity and confidence firmly rooted in humane goals that are currently lacking in too many of our societal institutions. Future generations of Americans must be educated for life in an increasingly complex world. Knowledge must be made available to the work force to keep America an economically vital place.

The danger is that, in attempting to respond to every need, community colleges may be distracted from the transcendent, integrative goals. Survival without a sense of mission can indeed be the forerunner of extinction. The ultimate loser would be a society that can no longer count on the cement that keeps it from falling apart, with people scattered into myriad unrelated cells, trained but not educated, sure of individuals' special desires and interests but ignorant of shared purposes and ideals.

At its best, the nation's community colleges should bring together the visions and experiences of all their parts to create something greater than the sum. They should offer the prospect that personal values will be clarified, that individual competence and confidence will be enhanced, and that the channels of our common life will be deepened and renewed. And, through continued education, students of all ages must be prepared to participate more effectively in civic life.

As these goals are vigorously pursued, the community colleges of the nation will fulfill, in new and creative ways, their traditional mission as "colleges of the people." In the end, community must be defined not only as a region to be served, but also as a climate to be created in the classroom, on the campus, and around the world.

We recommend, therefore, that *Building Communities* become the new, compelling challenge for the community colleges of the nation as they move toward the year 2000 and beyond.

NOTES

I. THE MISSION: BUILDING COMMUNITIES

1. References to the historical development of the community college are drawn from commissioned research prepared by Allen A. Witt.

2. Elaine El-Khawas and others, *Community College Fact Book* (New York: Macmillan, forthcoming).

II. PARTNERSHIPS FOR LEARNING

1. Joyce D. Stern, ed., *The Condition of Education* (Washington, D.C.: Office of Educational Research and Improvement, U.S. Department of Education, 1987), p. 26.

2. Center for Education Statistics, U.S. Department of Education. Unpublished data, 1988.

3. "Community, Technical, and Junior Colleges: A Summary of Selected National Data," issued by the American Association of Community and Junior Colleges, December 1987.

4. The Carnegie Foundation for the Advancement of Teaching, National Survey of Faculty, 1984.

5. American Association of Community and Junior Colleges, *New Staff for New Students*, p. 194.

III. CURRICULUM: FROM LITERACY TO LIFELONG EDUCATION

1. William B. Johnston, *Workforce 2000: Work and Workers for the 21st Century* (Indianapolis: Hudson Institute, 1987), pp. xix, xx.

IV. THE CLASSROOM AS COMMUNITY

1. Mortimer J. Adler, *The Paideia Proposal: An Educational Manifesto* (New York: Macmillan, 1982), p. 23.

2. Quoted in William McCleery, *Conversations on the Character of Princeton* (Princeton, New Jersey: Princeton University Press, 1986), p. 106.

VI. CONNECTIONS BEYOND THE COLLEGE

1. U.S. Bureau of the Census, "What's It Worth? Educational Background and Economic Status, Spring 1984," *Current Population Reports*, series P-70, no. 11, 1987.

2. References are drawn from "Community College Involvement in the Education of Adults," a survey submitted to The Carnegie Foundation for the Advancement of Teaching by Arthur Cohen, February 1987.

VII. LEADERSHIP FOR A NEW CENTURY

1. John W. Gardner, "The Task of Motivating," *Leadership Papers, No. 9*, Leadership Studies Program, Independent Sector, pp. 10, 14.

2. Elaine El-Khawas and others, *Community College Fact Book* (New York: Macmillan, forthcoming).

3. J.L. Wattenbarger and S.L. Mercer, *Financing Community Colleges, 1987* (Gainesville, Fla.: Institute of Higher Education, University of Florida, 1987).

4. Elaine El-Khawas and others, *Community College Fact Book*.